The Great War 1914-1918

A brief introduction to the causes of war in 1914 with a reference to they key issues of war and a collection of stories

Martyn Hale

DEDICATION

This book is dedicated to my parents who are no longer with me but always supported me in my interest and my career as a teacher. From a young age, they always encouraged hard work and for me to follow my dreams.

To Sandra and Alastair, thank you mom and dad.

CONTENTS

ACKNOWLEDGMENTS

Thank you to **www.WW1Photos.com** for the use of their images. Also thank you to Jeremy Banning who pointed me in the right direction for images.

Introduction

This book is an overview of the causes of the Great War 1914-1918, followed by a summary of important factors that need consideration and essays that would challenge just two issues, who is to blame for the outbreak of war and the issue of stalemate. This book also shares some short stories with you, a different take on the issues of war.

The Great War or the First World War dependent on your preference has been a passion of mine since I first went to the battlefields of Ypres in 1999 with my school, Aldersley High School in Wolverhampton. From this point on, at the age of 15 I was gripped with all issues surrounding the war. Part of my interest was ignited by my history teacher, he himself a Great War enthusiast. Over 20 years have passed and my passion for the Great War has remained, it features in my teaching and it is my hobby. Teaching the Great War and how it is done is a very personal thing for each teacher wanting to tackle this complex subject. Some teachers tackle it from a causes, battles, and treaties approach. Whereas other teachers may teach from a local point of view, involving the community experience of war. Some also teach the war through different characters and their experiences. Whether that be a local soldier, a Victoria Cross winner, nurses, Footballers such as Walter Tull or indeed soldiers of different backgrounds. Whichever approach a teacher takes, the important thing is that they are teaching it. The centenary has passed but my feeling is that the teaching of the Great War should continue. Making it more relevant each year.

Chapter 1: The Causes of the Great War 1914-1918

We will start with the facts and work back: it may make it all the easier to understand how the Great War happened. The events of July and early August 1914 are a classic case of "one thing led to another" - otherwise known as the treaty alliance system.

The explosive that was Great War had been long in the stockpiling; the spark was the assassination of Archduke Franz Ferdinand, heir to the Austro-Hungarian throne, in Sarajevo on 28 June 1914.

Ferdinand's death at the hands of the Black Hand, a Serbian nationalist secret society, set in train a mindlessly mechanical series of events that culminated in the world's first global war.

Austria-Hungary's Reaction

Austria-Hungary's reaction to the death of their heir (who was in any case not greatly beloved by the Emperor, Franz Josef, or his government) was three weeks in coming. Arguing that the Serbian government was implicated in the machinations of the Black Hand (whether she was or not remains unclear, but it appears unlikely), the Austro-Hungarians opted to take the

2

opportunity to stamp its authority upon the Serbians, crushing the nationalist movement there and cementing Austria-Hungary's influence in the Balkans.

It did so by issuing an ultimatum to Serbia which, in the extent of its demand that the assassins be brought to justice effectively nullified Serbia's sovereignty. Sir Edward Grey, the British Foreign Secretary, was moved to comment that he had "never before seen one State address to another independent State a document of so formidable a character."

Austria-Hungary's expectation was that Serbia would reject the remarkably severe terms of the ultimatum, thereby giving her a pretext for launching a limited war against Serbia.

However, Serbia had long had Slavic ties with Russia, an altogether different proposition for Austria-Hungary. Whilst not really expecting that Russia would be drawn into the dispute to any great extent other than through words of diplomatic protest, the Austro-Hungarian government sought assurances from her ally, Germany, that she would come to her aid should the unthinkable happen and Russia declared war on Austria-Hungary.

Germany readily agreed, even encouraged Austria-Hungary's warlike stance. Quite why we will come back to later.

One Thing Led to Another

So then, we have the following remarkable sequence of events that led inexorably to the 'Great War' - a name that had been touted even before the coming of the conflict.

- Austria-Hungary, unsatisfied with Serbia's response to her ultimatum (which in the event was almost entirely placatory: however, her jibbing over a couple of minor clauses gave Austria-Hungary her sought-after cue) declared war on Serbia on 28 July 1914.
- Russia, bound by treaty to Serbia, announced mobilisation of its vast army in her defence, a slow process that would take around six weeks to complete.
- Germany, allied to Austria-Hungary by treaty, viewed the Russian mobilisation as an act of war against Austria-Hungary, and after scant warning declared war on Russia on 1 August.
- France, bound by treaty to Russia, found itself at war against Germany and, by extension, on Austria-Hungary following a German declaration on 3 August. Germany was swift in invading neutral Belgium so as to reach Paris by the shortest possible route.
- Britain, allied to France by a more loosely worded treaty which placed a "moral obligation" upon her to defend France, declared war against Germany on 4 August. Her reason for entering the conflict lay in

another direction: she was obligated to defend neutral Belgium by the terms of a 75-year old treaty. With Germany's invasion of Belgium on 4 August, and the Belgian King's appeal to Britain for assistance, Britain committed herself to Belgium's defence later that day. Like France, she was by extension also at war with Austria-Hungary.

- With Britain's entry into the war, her colonies and dominions abroad variously offered military and financial assistance, and included Australia, Canada, India, New Zealand and the Union of South Africa.

- United States President Woodrow Wilson declared a U.S. policy of absolute neutrality, an official stance that would last until 1917 when Germany's policy of unrestricted submarine warfare - which seriously threatened America's commercial shipping (which was in any event almost entirely directed towards the Allies led by Britain and France) - forced the U.S. to finally enter the war on 6 April 1917.

- Japan, honouring a military agreement with Britain, declared war on Germany on 23 August 1914. Two days later Austria-Hungary responded by declaring war on Japan.

- Italy, although allied to both Germany and Austria-Hungary, was able to avoid entering the fray by citing a clause enabling it to evade its obligations to both. In short, Italy was committed to defend Germany and Austria-Hungary only in the event of a 'defensive' war; arguing that their actions were 'offensive' she declared instead a policy of neutrality. The following year, in May 1915, she finally joined the conflict by siding with the Allies against her two former allies.

The Tangle of Alliances

Such were the mechanics that brought the world's major nations into the war at one time or another. It's clear from the summary above that the alliance system was as much at fault as anything in bringing about the scale of the conflict.

What was intended as a strictly limited war - a brief war - between accuser and accused, Austria-Hungary and Serbia, rapidly escalated into something that was beyond the expectations of even the most warlike ministers in Berlin (and certainly Vienna, which quickly became alarmed at spiraling events in late July and sought German reassurances).

It's possible to delve deeply into European history in the quest to unearth the roots of the various alliances that were at play in 1914. However, for our purposes it serves to date the origins of the core alliances back to Bismarck's renowned intrigues, as he set about creating a unified Germany from the loose assembly of German confederated states in the 1860s.

Bismarck's Greater Germany

Bismarck, first Prime Minister of Prussia and then Chancellor of the German Empire (once he had assembled it), set about the construction of Germany through high politics judiciously assisted by war against Austria and France.

Appointed Prime Minister and Foreign Minister of Prussia by Kaiser Wilhelm I in 1862, Bismarck was consumed with a desire to achieve the creation of a German Empire out of the collection of smaller German states largely led by Austria's influence (another German-speaking nation).

His first step was to oust Austria as the prime influence among these German states. He achieved this by engineering war with Austria in 1866 over disputed territory in the duchy of Holstein (much against the wishes of his own Kaiser). The resulting war lasted just seven weeks - hence its common title 'The Seven Weeks War' - and ended with the complete dominance of the supremely efficient Prussian military.

In a peace mediated by the French Emperor, Napoleon III, Bismarck extracted from Austria not only Schleswig and Holstein, but also Hanover, Hesse, Nassau and Frankfurt, creating the North German Federation. As importantly, Bismarck had successfully displaced Austria in the spheres of influence over the many small German states.

Having assembled a united assembly in the north Bismarck determined to achieve the same in the south - and so unite all the German states under the Prussian banner.

How to achieve this? Bismarck resolved that war with the French, a common enemy, would attain his aims.

First, he needed to engineer a credible reason for war. Thus, in 1870, Bismarck attempted to place a Hohenzollern prince on the throne in Spain. Napoleon III, fearful of the prospect of theoretical war on two fronts - for the Hohenzollern prince was a relative of Kaiser Wilhelm I - objected.

Bismarck turned up the diplomatic heat by releasing, on 14 July 1870, a doctored version of a telegram ostensibly from the Kaiser to Bismarck himself, called the Ems Telegram. The effect of the telegram was to simultaneously insult both France and Prussia over their inability to resolve the dispute over the Spanish throne.

Napoleon III, facing civil revolt at home over quite unrelated matters, and receiving encouraging noises from his military commanders, responded by declaring war against Prussia five days later, on 19 July 1870.

Once again, as was the case against Austria, the Prussian military machine demolished the French forces. Napoleon III, who personally led his forces at the lost Battle of Sedan, surrendered and was deposed in the civil war that boiled over in France, resulting in the Third French Republic.

In the meantime, the Prussian forces laid siege to Paris between September 1870 and January 1871, starving the city into surrender. The consequences of the war were numerous. Aside from the usual territorial gains - France ceded both Alsace and Lorraine to Prussia and was forced to pay reparations (equivalent to around $1 billion today) - the southern German states agreed to an alliance with their northern counterparts, resulting in the creation of Bismarck's cherished German Empire.

Bismarck's Need for Alliances

Bismarck's creation of a unified Germany was of direct relevance to the outbreak of war some 43 years later, since it resulted in the assembly of the key alliances that later came into play.

For, having achieved his life's aim, Bismarck's expansionary plans were at an end. He had secured what he wanted, and his chief desire now was to maintain its stability. He therefore set about building European alliances aimed at protecting Germany from potentially threatening quarters.

He was acutely aware that the French were itching to revenge their defeat at the earliest opportunity - and the loss of Alsace and Lorraine to Prussia would prove to be a lasting sore. Indeed, the French plan for war in 1914, Plan XVII, was largely based around the recapture of Alsace and Lorraine in the shortest possible time - with disastrous consequences.

Britain's Splendid Isolation

Bismarck did not initially fear an alliance between France and Britain, for the latter was at that time in the midst of a self-declared 1870s policy of "splendid isolation", choosing to stay above continental European politics.

If not Britain then, how about Russia and, conceivably, beaten foe Austria-Hungary?

The Three Emperors League & Dual Alliance

He began by negotiating, in 1873, the Three Emperors League, which tied Germany, Austria-Hungary and Russia to each other's aid in time of war. This however only lasted until Russia's withdrawal five years later in 1878, leaving Bismarck with a new Dual Alliance with Austria-Hungary in 1879.

This latter treaty promised aid to each other in the event of an attack by Russia, or if Russia aided another power at war with either Germany or Austria-Hungary. Should either nation be attacked by another power, e.g. France, they were to remain - at the very least - benevolently neutral.

This alliance, unlike others, endured until war in 1914. It was this clause that Austria-Hungary invoked in calling Germany to her aid against Russian support for Serbia (who in turn was protected by treaty with Russia).

The Triple Alliance

Two years after Germany and Austria-Hungary

concluded their agreement, Italy was brought into the fold with the signing of the Triple Alliance in 1881. Under the provisions of this treaty, Germany and Austria-Hungary promised to assist Italy if she were attacked by France, and vice versa: Italy was bound to lend aid to Germany or Austria-Hungary if France declared war against either.

Additionally, should any signatory find itself at war with two powers (or more), the other two were to provide military assistance. Finally, should any of the three determine to launch a 'preventative' war (a euphemism if ever there was one), the others would remain neutral.

One of the chief aims of the Triple Alliance was to prevent Italy from declaring war against Austria-Hungary, towards whom the Italians were in dispute over territorial matters.

A Secret Franco-Italian Alliance

In the event the Triple Alliance was essentially meaningless, for Italy subsequently negotiated a secret treaty with France, under which Italy would remain neutral should Germany attack France - which in the event transpired.

In 1914 Italy declared that Germany's war against France was an 'aggressive' one and so entitled Italy to claim neutrality. A year later, in 1915, Italy did enter the First World War, as an ally of Britain, France and Russia.

Austria-Hungary signed an alliance with Romania in 1883, negotiated by Germany, although in the event Romania - after starting World War One as a neutral - eventually joined in with the Allies; as such Austria-Hungary's treaty with Romania was of no actual significance.

The Reinsurance Treaty

Potentially of greater importance - although it was allowed to lapse three years after its signature - Bismarck, in 1887, agreed to a so-called Reinsurance Treaty with Russia.

This document stated that both powers would remain neutral if either were involved in a war with a third (be it offensive or defensive).

However, should that third power transpire to be France, Russia would not be obliged to provide assistance to Germany (as was the case of Germany if Russia found itself at war with Austria-Hungary).

Bismarck's intention was to avoid the possibility of a two-front war against both France and Russia.

A decidedly tangled mesh of alliances; but the Russian Tsar, Nicholas II, allowed the Reinsurance Treaty to lapse in 1890 (the same year the new German Kaiser, Wilhelm II, brought about the dismissal of his veteran Chancellor, Bismarck).

Franco-Russian Agreements

The year after the Reinsurance Treaty lapsed Russia allied itself with France. Both powers agreed to consult with the other should either find itself at war with any other nation, or if indeed the stability of Europe was threatened.

This rather loosely worded agreement was solidified in 1892 with the Franco-Russian Military Convention, aimed specifically at counteracting the potential threat posed by the Triple Alliance of Germany, Austria-Hungary and Italy.

In short, should France or Russia be attacked by one of the Triple Alliance signatories - or even should a Triple Alliance power mobilise against either (where to mobilise meant simply placing a nation on a war footing preparatory to the declaration of hostilities), the other power would provide military assistance.

British Emergence from Splendid Isolation

Meanwhile, Britain was awaking to the emergence of Germany as a great European power - and a colonial power at that. Kaiser Wilhelm's successor, Wilhelm II, proved far more ambitious in establishing "a place in the sun" for Germany. With the effective dismissal of Bismarck, the new Kaiser was determined to establish Germany as a great colonial power in the pacific and, most notably, in Africa.

Wilhelm, encouraged by naval minister Tirpitz, embarked upon a massive shipbuilding exercise intended to produce a naval fleet the equal of Britain's, unarguably by far and away the world's largest.

Britain, at that time the greatest power of all, took note. In the early years of the twentieth century, in 1902, she agreed a military alliance with Japan, aimed squarely at limiting German colonial gains in the east.

She also responded by commissioning a build-up in her own naval strength, determined to outstrip Germany. In this she succeeded, building in just 14 months - a record - the enormous Dreadnought battleship, completed in December 1906. By the time war was declared in 1914 Germany could muster 29 battleships, Britain 49.

Despite her success in the naval race, Germany's ambitions succeeded at the very least in pulling Britain into the European alliance system - and, it has been argued, brought war that much closer.

Cordial Agreements: Britain, France - and Russia

Two years later Britain signed the Entente Cordiale with France. This 1904 agreement finally resolved numerous leftover colonial squabbles. More significantly, although it did not commit either to the other's military aid in time of war, it did offer closer diplomatic co-operation generally.

Three years on, in 1907, Russia formed what became known as the Triple Entente (which lasted until World War One) by signing an agreement with Britain, the Anglo-Russian Entente.

Together the two agreements formed the three-fold alliance that lasted and effectively bound each to the other right up till the outbreak of world war just seven years later.

Again, although the two Entente agreements were not militarily binding in any way, they did place a "moral obligation" upon the signatories to aid each other in time of war.

It was chiefly this moral obligation that drew Britain into the war in defence of France, although the British pretext was actually the terms of the largely forgotten 1839 Treaty of London that committed the British to defend Belgian neutrality (discarded by the Germans as "a scrap of paper" in 1914, when they asked Britain to ignore it).

In 1912 Britain and France did however conclude a military agreement, the Anglo-French Naval Convention, which promised British protection of France's coastline from German naval attack, and French defence of the Suez Canal.

Agreements Set, The Occasional Minor War...

Such were the alliances between the major continental

players. There were other, smaller alliances too - such as Russia's pledge to protect Serbia, and Britain's agreement to defend Belgian neutrality - and each served its part in drawing each nation into the coming great war.

In the interim however, there were a number of 'minor' conflicts that helped to stir emotions in the years immediately preceding 1914, and which gave certain nations more stake than others in entering the world war.

Russian War with Japan: Shock Japanese Victory

Ever since Russia declined Japan's offer in 1903 for each to recognise the other's interests in Manchuria and Korea, trouble was looming.

The Japanese launched a successful attack upon Russian warships in Korea, at Inchon, and in Port Arthur, China. This was followed by a land invasion of both disputed territories of Korea and Manchuria in 1904.

Among other set-pieces, the Japanese astonished the western powers by destroying the entire Russian fleet at the Battle of Tsushima (27-28 May 1905) for the loss of two torpedo boats - a humiliating Russian defeat.

The U.S. President, Theodore Roosevelt, mediated a peace agreement between Japan and Russia, one that resulted in material gains for Japan and with note being taken in Berlin of the fallacy of the myth of Russian "invincibility".

The scale of Russia's defeat in part contributed to the attempted Russian Revolution of 1905, and the battered and shaken Tsar, Nicholas II, was determined to restore Russian prestige (not least in the Romanov dynasty itself): and what better way to achieve this than through military conquest?

The Balkans, 1912: Italy Versus Turkey

Strife in the Balkans was nothing new. In 1912 it continued with war between Italy and Turkey, over the latter's African possessions. Turkey lost and was forced to hand over Libya, Rhodes and the Dodecanese Islands to the Italians.

The Balkans, 1912 (Part II): The First Balkan War

Turkey's troubles were not yet over. Having concluded peace with the Italians it found itself engulfed in war with no fewer than four small nations over the possession of Balkan territories: Greece, Serbia and Bulgaria - and later Montenegro.

The intervention of the larger European powers brought about an end to this the First Balkan War of 1912-13. Again, Turkey lost out, shedding Crete and all of its European possessions.

The Balkans, 1913: The Second Balkan War

Later in the 1913, conflict erupted again in the Balkans, as Bulgaria, unsatisfied with its earlier spoils, fought with its recent allies in an attempt to control a greater part of Macedonia; and when the so-named "Young Turks" - Turkish army officers - denounced the earlier peace as unfair.

Between May and July 1913 Bulgaria's former allies beat back the new aggressor, Bulgaria, and Romania captured the Bulgarian capital Sofia in August. Beaten and having surrendered on 10 August 1913, Bulgaria also lost Adrianople back to Turkey.

Troubled Peace in the Balkans

Despite the re-establishment of peace in the Balkans, nothing had really been settled and tensions remained high. The numerous small nations that had found themselves under Turkish or Austro-Hungarian rule for many years stirred themselves in nationalistic fervour.

Yet while these Balkan nations sought their own individual voice and self-determination, they were nevertheless united in identifying themselves as pan-Slavic peoples, with Russia as their chief ally.

The latter was keen to encourage this belief in the Russian people as the Slav's natural protectors, for aside from a genuine emotional attachment, it was a means by which Russia could regain a degree of lost prestige.

Unsettled Empires

Come 1914, trouble was not restricted to the smaller nations outlined above. The Austro-Hungarian empire was directly impacted by troubles in the Balkans and, under the ageing Emperor Franz Josef, was patently struggling to maintain coherence of the various diametrically opposed ethnic groups which fell under the Austro-Hungarian umbrella.

As such, the assassination of Franz Ferdinand by the Serbian nationalist secret society, the Black Hand, provided the Austro-Hungarian government with a golden opportunity to stamp its authority over the region.

Russia, ally of the Slavs - and therefore of Serbia - had been struggling to hold back full-scale revolution ever since the Japanese military disaster of 1905. In 1914, while the Tsar himself was reluctant, his government saw war with Austria-Hungary as an opportunity to restore social order - which indeed it did, at least until the continuation of repeated Russian military setbacks, Rasputin's intrigue at court and food shortages combined to bring about the long-threatened total revolution (which, encouraged by Germany, brought about Russia's withdrawal from the war in 1917).

Then there is France. Almost immediately following her defeat by Prussia in the Franco-Prussian War of 1870-71, together with the humiliating annexation by the newly unified Germany of the coal-rich territories of Alsace and Lorraine, the French government and military alike were united in thirsting for revenge.

To this end the French devised a strategy for a vengeful war upon Germany, Plan XVII, whose chief aim was the defeat of Germany and the restoration of Alsace and Lorraine. The plan was fatally flawed and relied to an untenable extent upon the "élan" which was believed to form an integral part of the French army - an irresistible force that would sweep over its enemies.

Germany's Path to War

As for Germany, she was unsettled socially and militarily. The 1912 Reichstag elections had resulted in the election of no fewer than 110 socialist deputies, making Chancellor Bethmann-Hollweg's task in liaising between the Reichstag and the autocratic Wilhelm, not to mention the rigidly right-wing military high command, next to impossible.

Bethmann Hollweg, who became most despondent, came to believe that Germany's only hope of avoiding civil unrest sooner rather than later lay in war: preferably a short, sharp war, although he did not rule out a European-wide conflict if it resolved Germany's social and political woes.

This outlook on life fueled his decision of 6 July 1914 - whilst the Austro-Hungarian government was weighing its options with regard to Serbia - to offer the former what has been commonly referred to as "a blank cheque"; that is, an unconditional guarantee of support for Austria-Hungary no matter what she decided.

Germany's military unsettlement arose in the sense that Kaiser Wilhelm II was finding himself largely frustrated in his desire to carve out a grand imperial role for Germany. Whilst he desired "a place in the sun", he found that all of the bright areas had been already snapped up by the other colonial powers, leaving him only with a place in the shade.

Not that Wilhelm II was keen upon a grand war. Rather, he failed to foresee the consequences of his military posturing, his determination to construct both land and naval forces the equivalent - and better - than those of Britain and France (with varying success).

However, his government and his military commanders assuredly did anticipate what was to come. A plan to take on both Russia and France, a war on two fronts, had long been expected and taken into account.

The so-called Schlieffen Plan, devised by former Army Chief of Staff Alfred von Schlieffen, had been carefully crafted to deal with a two-front war scenario. The plan, which very nearly succeeded, outlined a plan to conquer France, to knock her out of the war, on a 'Western Front', within five weeks - before, the Germans calculated, Russia could effectively mobilise for war on the 'Eastern

Front' (which they estimated would take six weeks).

It is often speculated - and argued - that the plan would have succeeded but for the decision of the then-German Chief of Staff in 1914, Helmuth von Moltke, to authorise a critical deviation from the plan that, it is believed, stemmed from a lack of nerve, and crucially slowed the path towards Paris - with fatal consequences (and which ended in static trench warfare).

Still, the German plan took no real account of Britain's entry into the war. The German government gave no credence to the possibility that Britain would ignore her own commercial interests (which were presumably best served by staying aloof from the conflict and maintaining her all-important commercial trading routes), and would instead uphold her ancient treaty of obligation to recover violated Belgian neutrality.

British Dithering

It is also suggested that Germany would have backed away from war had Britain declared her intentions sooner. Believing that Britain would stay out of the coming conflict, and would limit herself to diplomatic protests - after all, Britain was under no strict military obligation to France - Germany, and Austria-Hungary, proceeded under the belief that war would be fought solely with France and Russia.

The British Government, and its Foreign Minister, Sir

Edward Grey, attempted to mediate throughout July, reserving at all times its right to remain aloof from the dispute. It was only as the war began that the British position solidified into support for, ostensibly, Belgium.

Hence the oft-levelled criticism that had Britain come out clearly on the side of Belgium and France earlier in July, war would have been avoided: Germany would have effectively instructed Austria-Hungary to settle with Serbia, especially given the latter's willingness to co-operate with Austria-Hungary.

Whether this would have transpired given the German war machine's determination for war is of course unknown.

A Family Affair

The First World War has sometimes been labelled, with reason, "a family affair". This is derived from the reality that many of the European monarchies - many of which fell during the war (including those of Russia, Germany and Austria-Hungary) - were inter-related.

The British monarch George V's predecessor, Edward VII, was the German Kaiser's uncle and, via his wife's sister, uncle of the Russian Tsar as well. His niece, Alexandra, was the Tsar's wife. Edward's daughter, Maud, was the Norwegian Queen, and his niece, Ena, Queen of Spain; Marie, a further niece, was to become Queen of Romania.

Despite these familial relations - nine Kings attended Edward's funeral - European politics was all about power and influence, of protection and encirclement. Thus the tangled web of alliances which sprung up in the wake of the rise of the newly united German Empire in 1871.

The July Crisis 1914

The so-called "July Crisis" actually spans the period from the assassination of the Austro-Hungarian heir to the throne, Archduke Franz Ferdinand, on 28 June 1914, to the general declaration of war in early August.

Elements within the Austro-Hungarian government had been itching to strike at Serbia during the immediate pre-war years but had lacked a credible excuse to do so. Nationalist pan-Slav agitation within Serbia, and which Austria-Hungary suspected was encouraged by the Serbian government, served only to destabilise Austro-Hungarian influence in the Balkans.

An Excuse for War

The assassination of Franz Ferdinand provided the Austro-Hungarian government with a readymade excuse to launch what it believed would prove a limited war against the manifestly weaker Serbians. Ferdinand's death was in any event not greatly mourned either by the government or by the Emperor himself, Franz Josef, with whom he had never been close and with whom he was frequently in political disagreement.

The Austro-Hungarian Chief of Staff - and Commander-in-Chief - was Conrad von Hotzendorf. For years he had been pressing for 'surprise' attacks against Austria-Hungary's enemies, i.e. Serbia and Italy. With the murder of Ferdinand, he pressed the Foreign Minister, Count Leopold von Berchtold, to declare a state of war with Serbia. Both were united in requesting Franz Josef and Prime Minister Tisza to launch an attack against Serbia without first declaring war in early July, thus guaranteeing an element of surprise.

Tisza however argued that retribution against Serbia - whose implication in Ferdinand's murder had not (and even today has not) been proven - should be sought via diplomatic channels. Tisza was aware of the possibility that war with Serbia could rapidly escalate into a general European conflict as a consequence of the treaty system.

One Treaty after Another

For Russia was bound by agreement with Serbia to protect her in the event of attack. Further, the Dual Alliance between Germany and Austria-Hungary stated that if either found itself at war with Russia the other would enter the fray to provide assistance.

Similarly, the Franco-Russian Military Convention of 1892 provided for French assistance should Russia find itself at war with either Germany or Austria-Hungary. And Britain was in effect (as the result of a number of agreements) - although not technically -

bound to aid France should she be at war with Germany.

The Austro-Hungarians were inclined to believe, however, that Russia would limit herself to diplomatic vacillations rather than go to war with Austria-Hungary (and therefore with Germany, etc). Nevertheless, Tisza was keen to ensure that, should the unthinkable occur and Austria-Hungary actually found herself at war with Russia, Germany would prove willing to honour her treaty obligations.

Germany's Blank Cheque

Germany, who to all intents and purposes appeared to be spoiling for confrontation, offered what became known as "the blank cheque" to Austria-Hungary on 6 July. In this diplomatic communication from the German Kaiser, Wilhelm II, Austria-Hungary was promised unconditional support from Germany regardless whatever action Austria-Hungary decided to take in punishing Serbia.

There is little doubt that this note from Germany was the first clear indication that Germany was agreeable to war with - at least - France and Russia; she hoped however to avoid war with Britain.

Much encouraged by this emphatic show of support, Austria-Hungary issued an ultimatum to Serbia on 23 July that effectively revoked Serbia's national sovereignty.

The ultimatum, which was nominally intended as a means of apprehending Franz Ferdinand's murderers, was confidently expected to be rejected by the Serbians.

An Ultimatum to Serbia

Consequently, plans for war began to be set in place in Vienna. The Austro-Hungarian Emperor, who understood what issuance of the ultimatum inevitably meant, had to be reluctantly persuaded to approve its dispatch.

Astonishingly however, Serbia consented to virtually all of Austria-Hungary's demands bar a number of minor clauses. Dissent on these however was seized upon by Austria-Hungary as the necessary pretext for a formal declaration of war on 28 July 1914.

The Month of Holidays

It was unfortunate that events took place during the month of July - a holiday month when politicians and diplomats were away from their desks. By the time the Austro-Hungarian ultimatum had been issued on 23 July - and after a cooling-off period had been allowed by the Austro-Hungarians, who remained anxious to avoid a general conflagration - both the French Prime Minister, Rene Viviani, and President, Raymond Poincare, were away from France on a diplomatic mission to Russia. There, at St. Petersburg, they reaffirmed their support for the Tsar, Nicholas II, in his backing of Serbia.

Another power - Italy - was, as a signatory of the Triple Alliance, supposedly bound to assist Germany and Austria-Hungary in the event of war but had separately signed a secret alliance with France that effectively removed her from the equation. In any event, both she and Turkey gave every indication of being unwilling to become involved during the course of July.

British Disinterest?

With the dominoes starting to fall, it remained unclear what position Britain would take. The German Kaiser was inclined to believe that Britain would look to her interests first and foremost and remain above the fray - after all, she had no obvious quarrel with either Austria-Hungary or Germany, at least in this matter.

Nevertheless, Britain was practically committed to France's defence; and the French went to some lengths to ingratiate themselves with the British during July. Yet the British government was aware that in order to enter the war a better reason than vague commitments to France would be necessary in order to convince British public opinion.

In the event Britain's guarantee to maintain Belgian neutrality - agreed at the 1839 Treaty of London - served its purpose. Although there was much disagreement within the British political elite concerning war, it was this guarantee that brought Britain into the war on 4 August.

Public Disinterest

The general populace was, in most cases, largely unaware of the imminence of war until the end of the month. Enjoying the warmth of a golden summer, Europe's citizens turned their attention chiefly to news of more local importance.

However, with Austria-Hungary's ultimatum of 23 July - and her declaration of war with Serbia five days later, the approach of war was rapidly hastened. The day after Serbia received Austria-Hungary's declaration of war, 29 July, the capital Belgrade was placed under bombardment.

Mobilisation of Armies

Russia mobilised the following day, 30 July, as did Austria-Hungary. The French, unwilling to start hostilities themselves, and painfully aware that this might serve only to alienate British sympathies, chose to withdraw their troops some 10 km all along the German border.

On 31 July Germany demanded of Russia that she immediately demobilise, while requiring from France - with an answer expected within 12 hours - a declaration of neutrality in the event of war with Russia. Germany's justification - that of self-defence - was regarded dimly by the French government, who replied that France would act in accordance with her own interests.

Panic across Europe

With no answer received to Germany's ultimatum the next day from Russia, both Germany and France ordered mobilisation on 1 August. Stock exchanges panicked and many were closed. Later that evening Germany formally declared war with Russia, despite Wilhelm's twelfth hour panicked decision to try and abort the German invasion of Belgium and France (ignored by his Chief of Staff Helmuth von Moltke).

Germany delivered an ultimatum to Belgium on the evening of 2 August, requiring that she remain neutral while German troops occupied the country while en route for France. The following day the British Foreign Secretary, Sir Edward Grey, announced to Parliament that Britain would fight to defend Belgian neutrality if necessary. At last Britain had openly stated her position.

The Belgian King, Albert I, declared on 3 August his rejection of Germany's ultimatum. The next day, 4 August, German troops invaded Belgium. Britain demanded a "satisfactory" explanation from Germany to be delivered by 11pm (UK time) for her decision to march into Belgian territory at Gemmerich. When it was not forthcoming at the appointed hour, Britain completed the European line-up by announcing a state of war with Germany.

Popular Enthusiasm

Initial reaction to the news of war among the European populace was overwhelmingly enthusiastic, far more so than expected (particularly in Austria-Hungary, where the various nationalities came together in an unexpected show of patriotic unanimity).

The war was, by general, agreement, likely to be over by Christmas.

Chapter 2: How was the Great War 1914 to 1918 to be fought?

Every country was deeply affected by the war in some way. Over 60 million Europeans fought in the war, 7 million died, 21 million disabled or seriously wounded. 4 million women lost their husbands, 8 million children their father. In France alone 250 000 buildings were destroyed, 500 000 damaged, 6000 square miles of territory devastated. The total estimate of the entire cost of the war £260 billion. Such statistics beggar belief. How did such a catastrophe occur?

What were the war aims of the respective powers at the outbreak of the conflict?

A-H was the only country with a clear preconceived war aims in August 1914? What was it? The rest were involved primarily because they were concerned that to be neutral was more damaging. Thus, autumn 1914 saw most combatants clumsily formulating war aims after the conflict had begun.

In Germany, propaganda portrayed the war as an attempt to escape strangulation by the encirclement by jealous rivals and righteously claimed Germany was 'not driven by the lust of conquest'. However, the announcement of the 'September Programme' showed Germany's preoccupation with her west and east borders. It made claims for new territories and expansion. This has been viewed by historians like Fischer as proof of Germanys pre-war aims and intentions.

GB, French and Russian war aims were originally about survival as a Great power. However, the public demanded something more honourable. GB and France concentrated on the destruction of the aggressive force and 'international danger' that was Germany, the end of Junker militarism and the House of Hohenzollern. This would in turn ensure a Europe 'safe for democracy'. In addition to this were rather more self-serving aims of eliminating the German Navy and Empire overseas. This was less about democracy and more about GB's trading interests. Equally French demands for the return of Alsace Lorraine was about 'revanchism'. The aim of creating independent 'nation states' and dismantling of the Habsburg Empire came later. For Russia, the main aim was access through the Black Sea via the Turkish Straits of the Bosporus and Dardanelles.

Why did the war become a static one, a war of attrition?

Put simply, the German and French war plans failed. Both the Schlieffen Plan and the French Plan XVII were offensive plans, (how were these to work?) the emphasis being surprise attack. Victory would be assured within 6 weeks or so. However, both plans had significant flaws. Germany's Schlieffen Plan was a very rigid, detailed plan that was dependent on all or, at very least, most parts working to perfection without delays of bombed bridges, roads or valiant resistant. Yet despite these flaws, it very nearly worked. Belgium succumbed in 2 weeks and the French army was being held up at the Ardennes and in Lorraine with heavy casualties. The BEF was also in retreat although it had had some success in delaying the German advance at Mons. However, the main failing of the plan was the loss of nerve by Generals Kluck and Moltke. They decided to go east of Paris and not carry on round the west as the plan stipulated. They feared a break in the line and so took the conservative option of trying to encircle Joffre's retreating army. This led to the Battle of the Marne in Sept 1914. The BEF and French forces succeeded in halting the German attack but were not able to force them back. They had taken up exceptionally strong defensive lines by the River Aisne. In turn both sides fought to outflank each other so began the 'Race to the sea', reaching the Channel by Nov 1914. Thus the pattern of the next 4 years was set with an unbroken line of trenches from the coast to the Alps stretching over 400 miles. The 'war of movement' was brought to an end. The huge casualty rates (In some quarters up to 40%) and depletion of supplies/munitions led both sides to draw breath and 'dig in' for a form of warfare that neither had experienced nor planned for.

What role did new technology play?

This was the first really industrialised war where the

combatants had the capacity to wage war on a scale otherwise unimagined. Heavy artillery and machine guns had been used before but never with such deadly consequences. Hundreds of thousands of dead on all sides within a few months, even more injured or captured. Aircraft, gas and later tanks were all utilised. E.g. gas was used by the Germans in April 1915, just outside Ypres, for the first time. The machine gun was an effective defence against attack but was too cumbersome to be used as an assault weapon. None of the new technology brought a breakthrough in 1915, 1916 nor 1917. Whatever each side threw at the other, it seemed to absorb and withstand. The network of trenches (front, reserve and support plus all the communication trenches) ensured that an attempt to capture any part was going to prove very difficult. In addition to this the German strategy of withdrawing to high ground and building deep, concrete lined trenches meant that the GB and French forces had an almost impossible task.

Chapter 3: How did the Generals try to deliver the decisive blow?

Generals on all sides were under considerable pressure to develop a strategy that would win the war. Most of them were steeped in 19th century values and found the modern 20th century warfare unfamiliar but nevertheless endeavoured to find a way. Germany's tactic was to hit the southern town of Verdun on 21st Feb 1916 with 2 million shells. They captured 3km of ground in 3 days but Petain's defence was ultimately to go down as one of the greatest in military history. Units were regularly rotated so as not to become too exhausted or overwhelmed by the horrors they saw and supply lorries were keeping the forces going at a regular 14 second interval! The casualty list rose to 700 000 after the French counterattacked in October and December and regained all the earlier losses. The horrors of this particular encounter were seared on the minds of all those who had witnessed Verdun. Further west, The Allies launched their own massive offensive on the Somme with similar outcomes. These were the 2 monumental failures of 1916. Put simply, until 1 side had a distinct superiority at all levels military effectiveness, it was not possible to overcome the stalemate that was the Great War. For most of the war there was no distinct superiority. Both sides had strengths but also weaknesses. One cannot simply blame the generals for failing to find a break though as this was an unprecedented situation

What impact did the navies have on the war?

After the huge spending in the naval race in the 20 years or so before the war, it was expected that the great dreadnought would play a major role. Ironically, the early naval engagements made it clear the decisive role would be played by cheaper and less glamorous weapons e.g. The German U boat, U9, sank 3 British cruisers in Sep 1914 within a matter of minutes and HMS Audacious was sunk a month later by a mine. The Germans sought to launch raids on the British fleets in the Pacific and Atlantic oceans with considerable success led by Admiral von Spee's cruiser squadron. However, the British counterattacked in 1914/1915 and eventually put an end to Von Spee's fleet and the threat of surface attack. The GB enjoyed surface supremacy for the remainder of the war which was vital as it allowed 8.5 million Empire troops to be moved to the Western Front and enforced a crippling blockade on Germany and facilitated the conquest of Germany's colonies. It also enabled the transport of US troops and resources in 1917, which was to prove a decisive role in the eventual victory.

The one area where Germany did prove very difficult at sea was in submarine warfare. They were used, at their peak, to sink much merchant and Royal navy shipping equivalent to 1 in 4 ships leaving British ports by 1917. The British countered with a convoy system that was also costly but able to reduce losses which allowed GB to make good their losses in the shipyards. By the end of the war, new counter technology such as mines and depth charges were able to wipe out half of the German U Boat fleet. The submarine proved to be a flawed strategy especially after its role in sinking the US ship Lusitania which brought America into the war. It had been a dangerous weapon but ultimately a flawed one.

Chapter 4: Were the British soldiers of The Western Front 'Lions Led by Donkeys'?

The traditional answer to this question is simply yes! The scale of human devastation during World War One has often been blamed on incompetent leadership. However more recent analysis of the nature of warfare and how the war was led has brought this traditional view into question.

Who were the Generals?

The most famous (infamous!) was Field Marshall Sir Alexander Douglas Haig, the commander-in-chief, whose leadership of the British army from 1916 onwards has often been the most reviled of WWI generals

Former British PM, David Lloyd George, wrote in his memoirs in 1930 that Haig was 'brilliant to the top of his Army boots'. David Lloyd George's view sums up the attitude of many people towards Haig and other British generals of World War One. They were, supposedly, 'donkeys': moustachioed incompetents who sent the 'lions' of the Poor Bloody Infantry to their deaths in futile battles. Many popular books, films and television programmes (Blackadder goes forth!) echo this belief. The casualty list - one million British Empire dead - and the bloody stalemate of the Western Front seem to add credence to this version of events. But there is another interpretation.

One undeniable fact is that Britain and its allies, not Germany, won the First World War. Moreover, Haig's army played the leading role in defeating the German forces in the crucial battles of 1918. In terms of the numbers of German divisions engaged, the numbers of prisoners and guns captured, the importance of the stakes and the toughness of the enemy, the 1918 'Hundred Days' campaign rates as the greatest series of victories in British history.

Even the Somme (1916) and Passchendaele (1917), battles that have become by-words for murderous futility, not only had sensible strategic rationales but qualified as British strategic successes, not least in the amount of attritional damage they inflicted on the Germans. No one denies that the British Expeditionary Force (BEF) had a bloody learning curve, or that generals made mistakes that had catastrophic consequences. However, before dismissing the generals as mere incompetent buffoons, we must establish the context.

What kind of army fought in the Great War?

From 1915 to 1918 the BEF learned, in the hardest possible way, how to fight a modern high-intensity war against an extremely tough opponent. Before 1914, the British army had been primarily a colonial police force, small but efficient. By 1916 it had expanded enormously, taking in a mass of inexperienced civilian volunteers. Later still, it relied on conscripts. Either way, it was a citizen army rather than a professional force.

The generals, who were used to handling small-scale forces in colonial warfare, had just as much to learn about a type of war for which they were almost entirely unprepared. It is not surprising that in the course of its apprenticeship the BEF had a number of bloody setbacks. What was extraordinary was that, despite this unpromising beginning, by 1918 this army of bank clerks and shop assistants, businessmen and miners should have emerged as a formidable fighting force.

An inescapable fact of life for Haig and his predecessor as commander-in-chief, Sir John French, was that Britain was the junior partner in a coalition with France. Naturally, the French tended to call the shots, even though the British C-in-C was an independent commander. Thus, in July 1916 Haig fought on the Somme largely at the behest of the French, although he would have preferred to attack, somewhat later, in the Ypres salient where there were more important strategic objectives. At this time the French army was under heavy pressure from German attacks at Verdun. This reality of coalition warfare also helps to explain why Haig never contemplated halting the Battle of the Somme after the disastrous first day.

The one real achievement of the Anglo-French armies on 1 July 1916 was to relieve pressure on Verdun, as the Germans rushed troops and guns north to the Somme to counter the new threat. If Haig had called off the offensive on 2 July, he would have thrown away this advantage. Sitting back and letting Britain's principal ally's army be mauled was simply not an option for Haig. The alliance between France and Britain was always a somewhat uneasy one. Lack of co-operation, let alone British inaction in 1916, might well have caused the coalition to fall apart.

How did this army fight?

In 1914-17 the defensive had a temporary dominance over the offensive. A combination of 'high tech' weapons (quick-firing artillery and machine guns) and 'low tech' defences (trenches and barbed wire) made the attacker's job formidably difficult. Communications were poor. Armies were too big and dispersed to be commanded by a general in person, as Wellington had at Waterloo a century before, and radio was in its infancy. Even if the infantry and artillery did manage to punch a hole in the enemy position, generals lacked a fast-moving force to exploit the situation, to get among the enemy and turn a retreat into a rout.

In previous wars, horsed cavalry had performed such a role, but cavalry was generally of little use in the trenches of the Western Front. In World War Two, armoured vehicles were used for this purpose, but the tanks of Great War vintage were simply not up to the job. With commanders mute and an instrument of exploitation lacking, World War One generals were faced with a tactical dilemma unique in military history.

It is not true, as some think, that British generals and troops simply stared uncomprehendingly at the barbed wire and trenches, incapable of anything more imaginative than repeating the failed formula of frontal assaults by infantry. In reality, the Western Front was a hotbed of innovation as the British and their allies and enemies experimented with new approaches. Even on the notorious first day on the Somme, the French and 13th British Corps succeeded in capturing all of their objectives through the use of effective artillery and infantry tactics; the absence of such methods helps to explain the disaster along much of the rest of the British position.

How did warfare change between 1914 to 1918?

The problem was that in 1914 tactics had yet to catch up with the range and effectiveness of modern artillery and machine guns. Warfare still looked back to the age of Napoleon. By 1918, much had changed. At the Battle of Amiens on 8 August 1918, the BEF put into practice the lessons learned, so painfully and at such a heavy cost, over the previous four years. In a surprise attack, massed artillery opened up in a brief but devastating bombardment, targeting German gun batteries and other key positions. The accuracy of the shelling, and the fact that the guns had not had to give the game away by firing some preliminary shots to test the range, was testimony to the startling advances in technique which had turned gunnery from a rule of thumb affair into a highly scientific business.

Then, behind a 'creeping barrage' of shells, perfected since its introduction in late 1915, British, French, Canadian and Australian infantry advanced in support of 552 tanks. The tank was a British invention which had made its debut on the Somme in September 1916. Overhead flew the aeroplanes of the Royal Air Force, created in April 1918 from the old Royal Flying Corps and Royal Naval Air Service. The aeroplane had come a long way from its 1914 incarnation as an extremely primitive assemblage of struts and canvas, its task confined to reconnaissance.

By the time of the Battle of Amiens, aeroplanes were considerably more sophisticated than their predecessors of 1914. The RAF carried out virtually every role fulfilled by modern aircraft: ground attack, artillery spotting, interdiction of enemy lines of communication, strategic bombing. This air-land 'weapons system' was bound together by wireless (radio) communications. These were primitive, but still a significant advance on those available two years earlier on the Somme.

The German defenders at Amiens had no response to the Allied onslaught. By the end of the battle, the attackers had advanced 13km (eight miles) - a phenomenal distance by Great War standards. The Germans lost 27,000 men, including 15,000 prisoners and 400 guns. It was, the German commander Ludendorff admitted, the 'Black Day of the German Army'. From this point onward, the result of the war was never in doubt. Amiens demonstrated the extent of the military revolution that occurred on the Western Front between 1914 and 1918. It was a modern battle, the prototype of combats familiar to armies of our own times.

Conclusion

One cannot ignore the appalling waste of human life in World War One. Some of these losses were undoubtedly caused by incompetence. Many more were the result of decisions made by men who, although not incompetent, were like any other human being prone to making mistakes. Haig's decision to continue with the fighting at Passchendaele in 1917 after the opportunity for real gains had passed comes into this category. In some ways the British and other armies might have grasped the potential of technology earlier than they did. During the Battle of the Somme, Haig and Rawlinson failed to understand the best way of using artillery.

Haig, however, was no technophobe. He encouraged the development of advanced weaponry such as tanks, machine guns and aircraft. He, like Rawlinson and a host of other commanders at all levels in the BEF, learned from experience. The result was that by 1918 the British army was second to none in its modernity and military ability. It was led by men who, if not military geniuses, were at least thoroughly competent commanders. The victory in 1918 was the payoff. The 'lions led by donkeys' tag should be dismissed for what it is - a misleading caricature.

Chapter 5: Why were the Allies able to go from defeat in 1916 to Victory in 1918?

Probably the most important learning experience undergone on the Somme related to artillery. Even during the battle, some commanders learned the importance of concentrating artillery fire. Comparing the attack of 14-15 July 1916 to that of a fortnight before, we find two thirds of the guns firing at one eighteenth the length of trench. By the end of the battle, it was more widely accepted that German artillery batteries were themselves a prime target which had to be dealt with before and during an attack.

The Somme saw the one of the first uses of the 'creeping barrage', a wall of exploding shells which moved forward slowly over enemy trenches with infantry following close behind. It ensured the Germans stayed under cover until the British soldiers were upon them. In the early days of the Somme, these barrages sometimes moved too fast for the troops behind them, allowing the Germans to emerge from their bunkers and man their defences before the British arrived. But over the next two years the barrages would become increasingly sophisticated, incorporating different weapons and multiple variations in timing.

In the period after the Somme, British artillery became increasingly adept at using a variety of methods to bring their guns into action quickly, accurately and decisively.

These included dispensing with the practice of firing 'ranging shots' which gave the Germans prior warning of an attack, in favour of 'pre-registration' of artillery using a grid map system. Heavier guns - like the 12-inch howitzer below - and innovations in the shells designed for them allowed British artillery to perform a wide range of tasks, from destroying barbed wire to knocking out enemy guns.

How were the infantry utilised differently after 1916?

Before, during and after the Somme, British infantry were re-equipped with light machine guns and rifle grenades, as well as being able to call upon their usual pre-war weapons. As a result, while infantry battalions became steadily smaller throughout the war, the quantity of firepower they could produce became steadily larger. In the winter of 1916-1917, as a direct result of experience on the Somme, the infantry was formally reorganized to make the 'platoon' (40 men) the key tactical unit, rather than the larger 'company' (150 men). Platoon commanders were given control of these new infantry weapons, so that they had available both automatic fire (machine gun) and indirect fire (such as trench mortars). Compared to their predecessors, junior commanders - subalterns and non-commissioned officers (NCOs) - were expected by 1917 to exercise far greater control and initiative over the battle at a local level.

A new system of standard formations and drills, combining fire and movement, was promulgated throughout the army to make use of this devolution of weapons and responsibility. When combined with accurate artillery fire in sufficient quantity, these changes made it possible for British infantry in 1917 to regularly break into strongly defended positions.

A central problem the army experienced during World War One was the difficulty of co-coordinating different arms and taking advantage of fleeting opportunities. On the Somme, soldiers in the front line found it extremely hard to communicate with rear areas and supporting units. Both telegraph wires and human runners were very vulnerable to enemy shellfire. Even when local successes occurred - as they did even on 1 July 1916 - by the time news got back to headquarters it was too late.

The British recognised the problem of communications, and in December 1916 'signallers' were instructed to follow close behind the attack, burying cables connected in a 'ladder' system so that one break would not disable the network. In the photograph below from October 1917, Royal Engineers carry drums of telephone wire to connect units on the battlefield near Ypres. The British Expeditionary Force (BEF) began experiments with the use of radio (which doesn't require vulnerable cables) , but sets remained too bulky and temperamental to use extensively. In its planning for the Battle of the Menin Road in September 1917, 1st Australian Division specified seven different means of communication between headquarters and the front line, including telegraph and telephone, visual signalling, wireless, power buzzers, motorcycle dispatch riders, runners and pigeons. These developments did not solve the problem of communications, but they did make it more likely that messages would get through.

What impact did new weapons have on military successes 1917 to 1918?

Although artillery and infantry remained central to the successful fighting of battles, the British army also made use of many pieces of new technology. Some of these are well known - the tank, the airplane and poison gas all achieved considerable success at different points in the war - but others are less familiar.

Enemy barbed wire was a major problem for British forces on the Somme, and it was very difficult to destroy with conventional artillery fire, which often either left the wire unscathed or broke up the ground so severely that it became impassable anyway. In response, the British created the '106 fuse' which caused artillery shells to explode on the slightest contact and to expend their force horizontally rather than burying themselves in the ground. It was extremely effective at cutting barbed wire. Available in small quantities in 1916, it was in 1917 that it came into its own as a weapon against wire and troops.

No new weapon was a war winner in itself. World War One tanks, for example, were mechanically unreliable, desperately uncomfortable to fight in, and remained vulnerable to enemy artillery and impassable ground. The Germans quickly developed countermeasures to every Allied technical innovation. New technology had to be integrated with existing arms in order to achieve the best performance. It was not until the last year of the war that the British became truly adept at combining new weapons and tactics to break into and then break through the German lines. Although tanks were first used at the Battle of Flers on the Somme in 1916, they did not start to come into their own until the Battle of Cambrai, in November 1917, and were arguably only truly well integrated into 'all-arms' battles in the summer of 1918.

Why was intelligence gathering much improved after 1917?

Many of the most important technical developments of the war related to the gathering of information. The key role of the Royal Flying Corps (RFC), on the Somme and after, was to observe and correct British artillery fire. This meant not only carrying observers but attempting to identify and communicate with British forces on the ground. Throughout the war, aerial photography steadily improved.

The British developed a number of other sophisticated means for locating enemy guns, including flash-spotting (looking for the muzzle-flash from enemy artillery pieces) and sound-ranging (calculating the position of enemy artillery from their sound). Taken together, these improvements allowed the British to target German artillery far more effectively in 1917. This counter-battery fire was a crucial ingredient in British successes in the second half of the war.

Battles of attrition – as many engagements of World War One tended to be – often lack decisive results. Because of this, information about the enemy was also a means of deciding success or failure. This, in turn, could give Intelligence officers tremendous influence over command decisions. Although the intelligence branch of British General Headquarters expanded enormously in 1917, the year after the Somme, it often provided over-optimistic information about the state of German reserves and morale - factors which were much more open to interpretation than the location of enemy guns.

None of the British army's tactical and technical developments would have been of much use if soldiers did not have the equipment, weapons and munitions to put them into effect. The Battle of the Somme stretched the improvised system of British logistics almost to breaking point. Over the winter of 1916-1917, the way that the British managed supplies was completely reorganized, partly under the supervision of Sir Eric Geddes, a civilian brought in because of his pre-war expertise in railway organization. A new system of 'prediction' of where and when supplies would be needed, and a new emphasis on effective transport enabled British troops to fight more effectively. In particular, by 1917, British gunners were able to operate for the first time without serious restriction on the quantity of shells they could fire.

What changes were introduced to the training of British soldiers?

Even before the Battle of the Somme had begun, the British Expeditionary Force (BEF) had already made an effort to study its performance in battle and to learn from its successes and failures in 1915. This process of self-examination continued during and after the Somme. The British army had traditionally been suspicious of rigorously imposed doctrine, partly because of the sheer range of roles its pre-war soldiers had to fill, and partly because of strong traditions of regimental independence.

But the Somme demonstrated that standards of training - particularly in rifle fire - and methods in attack varied greatly throughout the army. Successful tactics developed by one unit were not necessarily spread throughout the BEF. In trying to turn a large number of civilians into soldiers quickly, the army found it necessary to standardise its procedures. From the summer of 1916 onwards, a series of training pamphlets were produced. They summarised the lessons learned on the Somme, laid down simple instructions for combat operations, and made sure that British soldiers adapted to the new demands of the modern battlefield.

In the last years of the war, General Headquarters in France paid particular attention to the training of its junior commanders.

Did the British army follow a steep learning curve to emerge victorious in 1918?

Military historians have come to talk of a 'learning curve' for the British army on the Western Front. This should not, however, necessarily be taken to mean a smooth progression of expertise. Many soldiers, at all levels of command, made mistakes or misinterpreted their experiences. Sometimes the wrong lessons were learned, or circumstances prevented the use of the most effective tactics. Given the high turnover of personnel, improvements could be hard to sustain. Yet we can point to individuals whose long-term experience of battle allowed them to adapt to the demands of the Western Front.

Rowland Fielding was an officer who served variously with the Coldstream Guards, the Connaught Rangers and the London Regiment from 1915 until the end of the war. On the Somme in September 1916, his battalion launched an attack which failed because the artillery preparation missed a German trench close to the British front line. Two years later, he wrote of the relationship between infantry and artillery:

The sense of comradeship and understanding between the two arms is almost perfect nowadays. Each appreciates the difficulties of the other's job ... It is generally better economy to risk a few casualties from our own fire than that the artillery should shoot too much for safety. More casualties may be caused in the attack by the machine guns of the enemy remaining in action between our infantry and our barrage, than are ever likely to result from accidents through closer shooting.'

In 1917, not least as a result of its experiences on the Somme, the British Expeditionary Force (BEF) developed the ability to regularly break into German defended positions. Given careful planning, abundant artillery support, and reasonable luck, the British were capable of making limited advances, while inflicting heavy casualties on their opponents. However, even successful operations still resulted in heavy casualties. It remained extremely difficult to convert initial tactical success into decisive victory. This was partly the consequence of contemporary technical developments in communications and transport, but mainly the result of the size, ability and determination of the opposing forces packed into a relatively small area of north-west Europe.

In the summer and autumn of 1918, the British were finally able to string together a sequence of victories which left German forces in disorganised retreat towards their own borders and played a major role the final victory. The massive German offensive of earlier 1918 had failed to achieve its objectives, and decisively weakened their army. At the same time, the British demonstrated their ability to fight battles making use of every arm - infantry, artillery, tanks, planes, cavalry and armoured cars - in which they not only broke into but broke through the German lines, as at Amiens on 8 August 1918.

The BEF also showed the logistical and organisational ability which enabled it to mount a series of such battles in quick succession. Arguably, this sequence of 'all-arms' battles was a crucial step in the development of modern warfare, and a remarkable achievement for the citizen army that had suffered on the Somme.

Chapter 6: Essays on the Great War

To what extent was Germany to blame for the outbreak of the First World War in 1914?

The outbreak of war in 1914 has been the subject of considerable debate ever since the war was concluded in 1918. Initially the victorious powers did blame Germany wholly for causing the war whilst historians from the 1920's and 30's tended to focus on the shared guilt e.g. Lloyd George argued that the nations of Europe slithered into the cauldron of war and nobody really wanted it but nobody really did anything to stop it. This argument has some credence but does not differentiate sufficiently between the Great Powers. Most had varying degrees of responsibility, not equal. The overwhelming evidence supports the argument that although Germany was not wholly to blame, she was certainly the most responsible. Their imperial, economic and military aggression had created flashpoints prior to 1914 but it was the calculated high risk gamble of Moltke, the Kaiser and his other chiefs of staff in July 1914 to exploit a local crisis in the Balkans between Russia and Austria Hungary that helped engineer a continental wide conflict that was to become the Great War. There is no doubt that great power relations had deteriorated from the 1890's onwards and the atmosphere in Europe was tense for many years running up to 1914. The claim therefore that the Anglo German naval arms race, the Alliances and the economic and imperial rivalry between the Great

Powers, all made war inevitable at some time.

This shared guilt argument does explain why it was possible or even probable for war to break out but it does not account for the timing of war and the accountability of individuals who took risks and made choices they were not compelled to make. European powers were used to settling disputes with each other and other less powerful countries through limited wars and therefore a war mind set was well established amongst the Great Powers.

The balance of power in Europe had been reasonably stable in the 19th Century but the emergence of Germany in 1871 began to challenge the existing order. Kaiser Wilhelm II ratcheted up the rivalry in the 1890's when he began to demand Germany's 'place in the sun' to create an Empire to rival that of Britain's and France. He also had ambitions to dominate international diplomacy through his policy of Weltpolitik. His zealous nationalism also brought Germany into conflict with Britain, Russia and France. Germany had calculated that her security would be best served by an alliance with 2 other continental powers. Thus, an alliance system emerged as the Triple /dual alliance between Germany, Austria Hungary and Italy. Russia and France also realised the value of an alliance, with Britain remaining on the edge, committing to very little until it really had too.

The alliance system coupled with the naval and military arms race meant that all Great Powers spent millions on strengthening their defences and preparing for possibility of war. There had even been instances in 1905 and 1911 where clashes between Germany and France came close to war over Morocco but war was averted. Equally the Balkan league wars of 1912 and 1913 were encouraged by alliances working together. It is also true that the Great Powers devised detailed war plans through the early part of the 20th century which again suggests an expectation of war in the near future. Germany's Schlieffen Plan in particular was conscious of the need to act decisively and speedily if war were to break out. However, this is not sufficient to explain why war broke out in August 1914.

The July Crisis of 1914 that was sparked by the assassination of the Archduke Franz Ferdinand on June 28th in Sarajevo did not initially raise alarm bells with all the Great Powers. A continental war was not inevitable even if a localised regional war in the Balkans was looking likely. Indeed, in France and Germany, leaders went off to enjoy their summer holidays. Austria-Hungary, however, was keen to exert its power in the region. It was the dominant Great Power in the region since 1908, much to the chagrin of the Russians, but it was facing strong Slavic nationalism from the Serbs in Bosnia and Serbia itself. Emperor Franz Josef wanted to deal with the Serbs once and for all and knew that if he started a war with them, then Russia may well get involved.

He knew they wanted to avenge the humiliations of 1908

when Austria had outwitted them. It was the call for German support that was pivotal in turning this local crisis into a European conflict. Germany issued a statement to Austria that was described as a 'blank cheque' and this emboldened the Austrians to issue their ultimatum to Serbia. This was simply pretence at resolving the dispute peacefully as Austria had no intention to follow a diplomatic route. If Germany had tried to advise Austria to do so, then it is unlikely that Austria would have gone alone and risked Russia getting involved.

There is no doubt that Austria and Russia did make prospect of war in the region possible, but it was Germany who ensured it became something much more. The key question, therefore, is why Germany provoked war knowing that it would lead to a wider conflict. The research of Fritz Fischer and his colleagues in the 1960's points to the need for war sooner rather than later. Germany was acutely aware that it was losing ground to Russia and France and that both would be much better prepared for war in 1915 and beyond than they were in 1914. This would put pay to any of Germany's long held ambitions. The Admiral Müllers diary entry and Moltke memorandum in 1912 both make clear that a 'war sooner rather than later' was inevitable. It would enable Germany to fulfil its foreign policy ambitions to be the dominant power in the world. It was also clear that the Schlieffen Plan's effort to avoid fighting on two fronts simultaneously would be defunct if both France and

Russia could mobilise quickly. Fischer also argues that a war was good distraction from the social and economic problems in Germany and would unite all Germans behind the Kaiser instead of challenging him.

Germany saw an opportunity to bring about a war and therefore the very high-risk gamble of the chiefs of staff to back Austria and to partially mobilise German forces set the train in motion. AJP Taylor described it as war by timetable and July 28th, 1914 is the key turning point when war became inevitable. It is true that other countries could have made different decisions and avoided war in 1914 but the balance of power would have shifted very favourably towards Germany. A situation none of the Triple entente could tolerate. Germany knew this and still Germany forged ahead. The Kaiser's argument that Britain would not risk war with its 'contemptibly small army' over a little scrap of paper' to defend Belgium neutrality was naive at best. Germany wanted a war and Germany engineered the situation to provoke war. The Kaiser's long held ambitions for imperial, military and political dominance provided the coals for war and the Balkan crisis of 1914 provided the spark. Therefore Austria, Russia and Serbia should some responsibility for causing a localised regional war but Germany shoulders the most responsibility for a European wide conflict we know as the Great war.

Assess the reasons why the stalemate on the Western Front was finally broken by 1918

1918 was the breakthrough year in the Great War and the stalemate was finally broken. Some of the contributing factor for this include improved technology, changes in tactics and strategy. However, this alone does not explain why it was ultimately the Western powers that broke the stalemate. In fact, Germany had been the first in 1918 with their 'last gamble' to try and break the stalemate and came very close to smashing through the Allied line. Why did the Allies succeed in breaking the stalemate where Germany failed? The answer lies predominantly in the long-term impact of the on-going Allied naval blockade and the arrival of the USA.

The physical and psychological impact of the naval blockade was most acutely felt in 1918 as was the USA's arrival on the battlefields of the Western Front. Germany was starved of essential materials, resources and energy supplies. The failed Spring offensive and the counterattack launched in August 1918 meant Germany had finally exhausted herself in every sense of the word. The lessons learnt in terms of tactics and strategy coupled with an improvement in weapons technology meant the Allies were able to exploit Germany, and this opportunity, as never before. The Allied blockade had destroyed Germany's ability to wage war, as it had also done to her allies, and the USA's arrival demolished whatever morale was left.

In the spring of 1918, General Ludendorff ordered a massive German attack on the Western Front to try and break the stalemate. The Spring Offensive was Germany's 'last gamble' to end the stalemate and win the Great War. Ludendorff recognised a very small window of opportunity to successfully win this war and timing was everything. With 500,000 troops added to Germany's strength from the Eastern Front after the surrender of Russia and the Treaty of Brest Litovsk, Ludendorff was confident of success. Along with this, Germany wanted to launch an attack before the Americans fully established themselves in France. Germany needed to make a clear advance and gain significant territory before America could send more troops. The success of the Spring/Ludendorff offensive would also quell the ever-growing discontent within Germany. This combination of factors forced Germany's hand into this last gamble to break the deadlock and secure victory.

German tactics, including the deployment of heavily armed storm troopers, who "moved like snakes", and highly accurate artillery, meant huge gains in the first few days and weeks of the offensive. However, the Entente powers had also learned to retreat to better terrain to defend. This was key change in tactic that meant the line bent but never broke. This was in contrast to the mistakes in previous years

A really important factor that enabled Britain to take

advantage of the exhausted German army was the constant supply of reliable equipment. This was in stark contrast to Germany's increasingly depleted reserves. Britain was producing more tanks, aircraft and artillery shells and guns in 1918 than at any point in the war. In 1918 the Allies had 4000 tanks as a result of a national campaign to support the tank. The Germans on the other hand had a meagre 500.

The BEF was also better trained and morale was high when it became clear Germany could not sustain its offensive. A good example of this was at the Battle of Amiens in August 1918. The BEF brought the 'all arms' battle to the Western Front, something that would not have been foreseen in the early citizen army. Three years of battlefield experience was key to sustaining success. This combination of training and the more reliable and accurate technology were important factors as to why the stalemate was finally broken in 1918. These soldiers were well armed with light machine gun and trench mortars which enabled them to attack quickly and to sustain it. They were also very well supported by 10 000 aircraft and much improved communication and intelligence gathering. This was five times Germany air force which stood at a paltry 2 000.

The counter offensive in the summer and autumn of 1918 that broke the stalemate differed to previous offensives in that the western allies were able to sustain the attack and keep the momentum going. The 100 days after August 8th led to the most successful British military campaign of the war and indeed of any previous conflict. Ludendorff at the time described it as the 'blackest day' in German history.

Why was it possible for the Entente powers to soak up such a massive offensive and then launch a successful counter offensive whilst Germany could not? The most important factor was supplies. The convoy system at sea ensured that supplies got through to Britain. The German U Boat campaign was not able to inflict significant damage to the convoys after 1917 whilst in stark contrast; Germany's war machine was strangled by the Allied blockade both at home and on the Western Front. Equally the total mobilisation in Britain was not matched in Germany e.g. use of women in the workforce was not replicated in Germany.

The severe winter of 1917/ 18 exacerbated Germany's troubles and abilities to manufacture and to supply the frontline – food, fuel, medical supplies and ammunition were all in very short supply. This was due mainly to the long-term effects of the Allied blockade. The psychological effect was demoralisation and discontent at home. This rippled through to the frontline and forced Ludendorff's hand into his 'last gamble'. It also meant that once the assault was held up, Germany had nothing in reserve. Retreat to the highly fortified Hindenburg line was simply a temporary and short-lived reprieve.

The entry of the USA at the same time as the Blockade was biting hardest, is an extremely important cause of the stalemate being broken. In both defence and counterattack the Americans showed they were willing to make heavy sacrifices for victory. In proving their fighting ability, they also inspired the veteran French and British troops to heroic efforts in stopping the Germans. An example of American battle honours would be their drive north along the Meuse Argonne rivers. Without the logistical support and man power of the Americans coupled with their vital supplies across the Atlantic, the BEF would have found it difficult to make the advancements on the Somme in 1918, advancements which resulted in 100,000 German soldiers being taken prisoner of war, and the ultimate result being the Germans in full retreat.

More importantly than the USA's practical help was the psychological effect on the German army. It became quite apparent by the late summer of 1918 that the USA could reinforce its own men and supplies indefinitely whilst Germany could not. This was critical in breaking Germany on the Western Front and was key to so many soldiers surrendering and mutinying. The arrival of the USA was the trigger that finally broke Germany's will to fight on.

Ultimately the end of the stalemate in 1918 was a combination of factors. Germany's desperate last gamble and the Allies much improved strategy of retreat coupled with a better deployment of troops and technology in counterattack made the difference on the battlefield. However, without the long-term impact of the Allied blockade and the impact of the USA, the opportunity to break Germanys defence would not have appeared and it is likely the stalemate would not have been broken in 1918. For so long both sides had been evenly matched but by 1918 they most definitely were not.

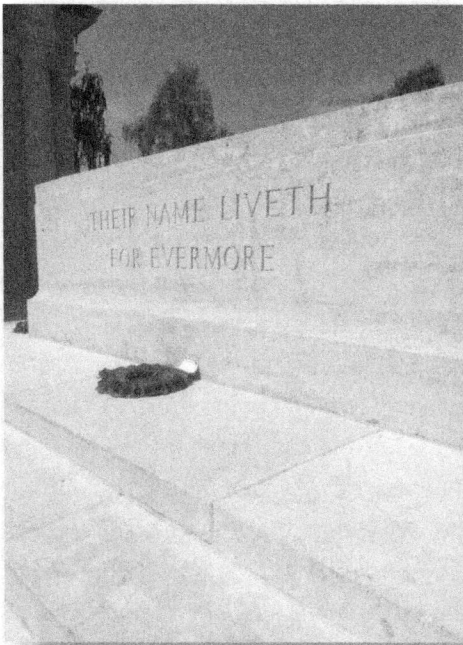

Chapter 7: Collection of Fictional Stories

The Shadow Writer

Before we start this, I need to tell you something, three something's to be precise. Firstly, ever wondered what it's like to be dead but still in the land of the living? Well, let me tell you now, because I have first-hand experience, it's nothing like being a zombie! There is no one alive or dead for that matter that I want to hurt, or suck brains from for that matter. But it's not much fun either. The people you love die and for some reasons you don't go where they go. You see all you know change and the things you cared about are no longer important to everyone else. Or worse - other people change them. History has a way of changing to fit the present. We twist and turn the past to suit until it is unrecognisable to those who lived through it and then what really happened is forgotten, ridiculed or changed. I should know - I've lived through history and then seen the rest of it. Being like this, dead but not gone, is like being part of a shadow. You know when the sun shines at the end of an autumn day and you know there is a long shadow behind you? That's what I feel like some days, that shadow. People can sense me there. They know something is with them, but they take little notice. I am a shadow person, I don't know why, I only know I have been wandering this earth now for nearly 100 years. Very soon it will be the century of my death.

I was killed during the First World War and for some reason I have not gone where everyone else has gone. Believe me I have looked everywhere and followed death. I waited while people died. I was there when my Mam died and Lizzy, Frank and our Jo, Uncle Dafydd and Evan, all my family grown far and wide. And all my pals (the ones I could find anyway), who had survived the war and tried hard to live a normal life I was there with them when they died. But no one ever heard me or sensed me near, or if they did, they never said anything. I searched out death. I would wait and hope that someone's death could bring answers about mine. At first, I would try and help them, I would tell them comforting things, so they would know it's not the end. But they could not hear me. And when they died, I don't know where their shadow went. Sometimes people responded to me when I talked but not in a good way, let's just say it was not beneficial to them. They got scared hearing my voice and thought they were going mad. This is not the best thing to happen to you before you die, hearing a man with a slight Southern Welsh accent, hoarse from years of smoking talking to you. And I am not the most expressive in times of difficulty. I suppose 'It's not so bad on the other side' is not the most reassuring sentence you would want to hear when you are about to die!

So, I waited and watched as people died. I hoped someone, somehow would produce a shadow like me, or I would find someone to help me find some answers to why I am like this. I went everywhere at the start. I went to the places I had been, to the Somme, to Ypres, even the British Channel - across and under on doomed vessels. But no one or nothing came for me, so I continued to search. I have travelled around hospitals and institutions and waited with ex-soldiers as they died of hunger. The years went by so fast they seemed like minutes. I went back to the battlefields when they put all the monuments for the dead there. I hoped, like the Longstaff painting, that they would return, and I could be at peace. But it was not to be. I then lived through more war, still searching for answers. I went to Dunkirk and Belsen, Hiroshima and London as well as travelling the oceans and the skies. This time the years felt like centuries. After witnessing Korea and Vietnam, something changed inside of me; my shadow seemed to be growing dim, like a Toc-H lamp. I grew so weary. I had sought and searched but I knew I was not going to find another shadow like me. So, for a long time I was still, I was tired, I felt washed up and exhausted. I was brittle and despondent so I laid down in a wood which was close by where I used to live and hoped the earth would swallow me like it should have done all those years ago.

But I awoke again. Was it months or years later? I do not know how long I had slept on the earth and leaves. It did not matter to me anymore; time had no meaning for me. I had concluded that for some reason this shadow of me was my soul and I was doomed to wonder the earth, only a spectator for the big moving picture of life. That's what it is like being a shadow. You just watch the world. I can't participate so I observe. I see the horror and the beauty - it's really that simple to me. The horror is easy to see, and people always get distracted by it, I did too. For the first 50 years after my death all I did was follow war. That's not to say beauty does not exist in war, it does, it's just a lot harder to find. But there's a lot of horror and it's getting worse. When I went to war, we saw very little civilian casualties but now, more women and children are killed than soldiers and the new ways they think up to make people suffer never fails to frighten and dismay me.

The beauty of the world seems to be the most difficult for humans to see. I have grown to see the beauty that most people walk past; you can even find some of it in war. The sound of a bird singing when the guns stop, the sun rising when you Stand To and the trees swaying in the wind, all these I have seen in war. Not far from war is the sound of the sea, or a kiss from a lovely lady, the feel of warm rain, a smile, a cat sitting on a lap, singing with pals, marching, making a breakfast, a glass of beer. I could go on, all about the things I like, the things I look out for now, but I know you are not interested because these are my things. Next time you have a minute just imagine you have just a short time left on this earth. Who would you miss and what would be the beauty you missed the most?

So, I watch. I am not seen; well I don't think I am. In some instances, I have thought certain people have seen me.

Once there was this ex-soldier from the First World War in an institute for shell shock who seemed to talk to me like he knew I was there. I had found myself in this place because I was looking for an old pal of mine who I knew had suffered with his nerves and had been sent to a hospital, but I did not know which one. So, I searched for him in every town, in every hospital, institute and home but I never found him. But I found this fella who talked to me. He would look right at me and say stuff like 'Is that all you do? Stand there and stare?' And 'If I was you, I would tidy up that bloody uniform, it looks like you died in it.' I never said anything back; I was too scared in case he did not hear me, then I would really know he did not see me, or worse still start telling me off about how I looked and what I was doing. Frank, my pal - when he died many years after the war (he survived it all but many times I wished he hadn't), I waited by his bedside and watched him take his last breath. And that was it, he was gone but no shadow or soul or shadow soul or whatever I am. Several kiddies have often stopped, pointed and stared, asking their Mam's who that man is, but mothers are often in a rush and just move on. More recently there is this woman who seems to know I am there. Her name is Elly and she lives in my Mam's s old house, that's how come I know her. She sits and seems to ask me questions but as, yet I have not responded, am still not sure what she 'sees'. She says things like 'Why are you here?' and 'Can I help'? She also has lots of cats but my Mam always told me to stay clear of with women with cats as they were 'seers', I think she meant some sort of clairvoyance but I was never sure and she would tell me to 'Shhh now' and never said much more about it.

There is one other person who appeared to see me, but I made every effort to avoid him, as he just seemed to sneer at me. It was like he knew I was there, looking for answers and he could not believe how stupid I was because I did not know what or who I was. He made me uncomfortable though, I felt I knew him, but I could not stay and stare because he would sense me, look up and sneer. So, I stopped going to where he was, at the museum where he worked. I used to go there to read the old books on display under the cases there and they would change the pages every day. It was a long time ago, so he's probably dead now. No one talks about him at the museum and the books under the cases have all gone now, replaced by screens. I have not thought of him for a long time and I only mention it because he's the only person, since I have died, who ever made me feel uneasy, scared even. Even when I use to see horrendous things being done by people, I always felt like I was watching a moving picture and the people in it were actors. But with him it was different, he did not do anything bad, but he radiated evil. I used to think he might be working for the devil and I called him the shadow catcher.

I can smell, which is a blessing. Baked bread, summer meadows and autumn fires are my favourite. I must eat.

If I don't eat, I feel like thin paper left in the sunlight that gets brittle and parched. The only things I can eat are from the earth - and I have learned the hard way on this. If it's grown in the earth, and it's fresh, then that's fine. I live off vegetables, berries and fruit. I don't need much; a carrot can keep me going for days.

I once tried some chocolate because I really liked the stuff when I was alive, but it made me so weak I could not move. I really believed it was going to finish me off and take me to where I needed to go. It knocked me out for months. The weird thing about all this is that I still need to sleep, it's like a recharge for the shadow. I don't ever dream, or I can't remember if I dream. Sometimes I might have a feeling just after I have woken up that I was back with my pals or fighting in a certain place or being a young boy. But it's only ever a feeling, nothing more, just a flicker of my last life, fleeting. If I don't sleep and try and go without it, I just stop and when that happens, I can wake up anywhere. Once I tried to see how long I could last without sleep during the Battle of Britain, I lasted three weeks then woke up beside a loch in Scotland. There may be a connection to this but as, yet I can't figure it out. So, you get an idea of what I am or at least what I think I am. A dead man who searches the earth trying to find the reasons I am still here. Here as a shadow.

The second thing you need to know is that for the best part of my life I was a soldier, I fought before and during the Great War, and I really enjoyed the job. Let me say that again: I really enjoyed the job. When I was a young man many people had problems with this, they thought you were very strange wanting to be a soldier and even enjoying the job. But all that came about during the Great War, before that they never thought about soldiers or what they went through, they didn't give two hoots. We as soldiers we were the scum of our society and that was that. The public saw us as a nasty type of police force as we only ever 'came out' when there were strikes or riots to help the Bobbies.

And politicians and Royalty alike feared us in case we decided to turn our arms on them! No one ever thought about all the things we protected for the Empire, the land and borders, people and their Estates, trade routes and land shipments. No one cared about that; but let me tell you if we didn't care and if we didn't do our job, then England would not have had an Empire. The ships might have conquered the territory but we protected the Empire.

I can tell you how bad it was for soldiers then by the way they were treated when they come home and were too old to fight. Soldiers had to beg. When I was a young boy old soldiers would go from house to house begging. There were two in particular I remember. One was known locally as Bertie Buck, who would visit us a few times a year begging. He would stand outside the gate and shout up the path 'I got hit real bad, real bad I did, anything going? I got hit real bad I did Sir, anything going?' and he would pound his fist into his hand, not out of anger more anxious than anything. He had a dark complexion, possibly due to his current situation but he had bright blue eyes and a very English accent. He wore layers and layers of dirty clothes and had grubby medals on his chest, yet he never talked about what wars he fought in or even where he came from.

People said he had fought in the Crimean as he was known to mumble about Sebastopol and Inkerman, but no one knew for sure and he had a look about him, kind of a 'crazy but holding it together' look. You knew if you asked him about being a soldier, he would just go crazy. Then there was Mr Lawrence, or us kids use to call him Jumping Jack, who was a local man from Longhope who had joined the colours with a wave of patriotism. Before he knew where he was, he was involved in the Mutiny at Cawnpore, where women and children were butchered and cut up into pieces. He had a nervous breakdown. When we came back he was a changed man, or so I was told, he had lost nearly double his weight, and his trousers were gathered together with a piece of string, he had no teeth and took to shouting at himself and jumping at shadows. These were the regular beggars that I remembered; others would come through on their constant march for food. Lonely men who would not look you in the eye, asking if you had 'morsel or scrap for an ex-soldier mam'. They were allowed to beg; this is what this country gave them for fighting their wars and keeping their borders safe. Not a decent pension or somewhere to live but the right to beg. So, you can see what I mean, soldiers meant nothing. We could do all the dirty work, but your average person did not want to know about it and would not give us a second glance. To be honest, when I first joined the colours that suited me fine; I could get on with my job. Then it all changed. When the war started everyone loved soldiers and we could do no wrong and people cried 'it was time society treated us better', the 'good old soldier, who protects us from our enemies'. I could not believe how well we were treated; I could have been blown over by a feather. Women would give up their seats for us on the train and tram, offer to share their luncheons with us and tell us what brave and noble men we were. Old men would come up and shake our hands, pat us on the back and offer to get us some refreshments or give us some fatherly advice. The change came about because the war was very close; this was not Africa or Crimea but just over the channel. The changes were fast (this is the second reason why we became so popular) because lots of civilians joined the army in a hope to end the war soon. Lots of volunteers joined up, everyday folk, men who were clerks, university students, factory workers, train drivers, newspaper men, costermonger, rat catchers, night watchmen, chimney sweeps, dustmen, house breakers, teachers, labourers, farmers, shop assistants, carpenters, masons, smithies, gardeners, butlers, road sweepers and engineers, as well as criminals, under-aged lads and men on the run from various problems that included, but not limited to, women, gambling debts, madness and drink, all joined up. At the start we were flavour of the month, and if you did not wear a uniform you were ostracised, ignored, taunted and shamed by society for being a coward.   But that all changed. The war dragged on and on, and it did not end quickly. More men were dying or getting wounded than people believed possible. There was also conscription and young lads did not have a choice then. The war had become ugly and for that who do you think got the blame? Yep that's right, the soldiers. Not outright, that would not be allowed as we still had to fight and end the war, but more and more attitudes started to change. No one really wanted to know about what was happening in the war for soldiers. How bad some of the conditions were for some men, and not all the bad conditions caused by the war. The shells we got sent over from the factories in Britain for a long time were bad. They either went off before they were fired, fell short of where they should have gone killing British soldiers or landing and not exploding on the Germans. Some of the food we used to get sent over was appalling, not even edible and some people were making a lot of money from trades like this. Another thing was the dead and wounded, people at home suffered, they grieved their dead and tried to care for their wounded so there was very little left for us, we just had to be grateful we were not dead, maimed or mad, we were 'blessed' because we survived. We became the lucky ones but there was a lot of resentment about this from some people, it got worse as the war progressed and when it ended only the dead got remembered. But that's another story. Don't get me wrong, being a soldier is not an easy task and there were some parts of it I hated doing.

Some fatigues are soul destroying, you try cleaning up a make-shift latrine after 150 men have been using it or carrying barbed wire along a communication trench during a show or dealing with a soldier who has gone mad. Some of our equipment was so bad it did not work and was so old that it should have been in a museum. Some of the injuries and illness we had to deal with were very bad, particularly if you did not have a strong stomach. A man hit by shrapnel in the stomach was difficult, the first time I saw it I could not believe how much stuff came out of a human body, there was loads of it, not only blood but intestines of all shapes and sizes, bits of organ, stuff that looked like pus, food and bile and I see what I think to be faeces. That's not the worst of it. Many times, I have seen this happen and the man was still alive, holding what was left of his stomach and knowing the only thing coming is a painful death.

It sounds crazy but you hoped when you got hit that it was a quick one in the brain or heart and you knew little about it. Killing someone was hard, for any man who was not crazy or that way inclined, it was a difficult part of the job, but it's only a small part. It was made easier because often you knew if you did not kill them, they were going to kill you, you were protecting yourself, it was as simple as that. You have two or three men running down a trench towards you with all manner of weapons. You can try and run and get a bullet or bayonet in your back or you fight back, shoot to kill if you can or fight with anything you can get your hands on. We fought for what we believed in - peace. We did not want a big military country ruling our neighbours or us. The war was hard, but all wars are hard. You fight to protect what you believed in, a safe world. Funny because that often seems to be forgotten now. People seem to conveniently forget is that many of us fought for something we believed in and that never changed. To us the Germans were bad, they were trying to take over Europe and we knew we would be next. They did some terrible things those Germans, or some of them, but they had to be stopped and we stopped them. Don't ever forget that, we stopped them.

So, what's good about being a soldier? The things I liked were my pals, the army food, travelling and seeing new places, you feel like you have done a days work and every day is different. When you went to the front line as a soldier you only stayed there for an allocated amount of time then you would swap with another Battalion of men who would take over. When you were not in the trenches you could be doing a hundred different things, resting, fatigues, marching, training, fixing things, searching for things, drinking, eating, a concert, having a bath, it was always different. Also the trenches were all different, some were nice and quiet and very little happened, others were badly made and dangerous to work in, some were temporary, others had problems like water that would form pools of mud and slime and cause no end of misery. Some trenches were full of rats, some might smell due to old corpses that could not be removed or used to stable the trench wall (gross I know but once you're gone, your body might as well be doing something useful). There could also be left-over gas hanging around in trenches; this could be the smelly kind like mustard gas or the not-so-smelly kind like Phosgene, which would start working many hours after an attack by embedding itself into a man's lungs.

Other times, when we had attacked successfully we took over trenches from the Germans, which were very nice or if we got moved into a different sector of the line we would relieve the French whose trenches were not so nice, in fact they were very shabby. So you can see, always different.

You also moved about a lot. Sometimes you would stay in part of the line for a while and you would have so many days in the trenches there, then time out of the trench doing manual work and then some rest! If you had some good men opposite you, coming in when you were leaving you could get the trenches tidy and working well. Sometimes though you could have some lazy buggers opposite you, and you must tidy up after them all the time. To be honest, working on fatigues could be more dangerous than being in a trench. You see, trenches were built to withstand bombardments, as much as they could. But if you were taking provisions or equipment up to the front line it was much more dangerous as you were moving about in the open often carrying something very awkward. I remember carrying some gas bottles up before the Battle of Loos and it was a nightmare. They were really hard to carry because they were long and thin and difficult to get round the communication trench as it was meandering, dark and slippery and we were being shelled (if I remember rightly, by our own troops - as the shells fell short!). I learnt new swear words that night than I could have ever imagined existed! And some soldiers did not even fight, like the band men who became stretcher-bearers carrying the wounded, or the company cook. You know one of the things that I find hard to understand now is how people believe that when you were a soldier in the Great War all you ever did was live in trenches. Not true. Firstly, lots of lucky men had 'soldier' jobs away from trenches at base or at HQ. If they were really unlucky, they either went to sea or a few went in the air, and then if you thought a soldier's life was bad it was nothing compared to the miners.

And it did not matter if you were still home or mining where the fighting was, being a miner was a hard and dangerous job and it was all the time. The first job I had was down the pit and I hated it, I wanted out the first time I went down there. Dirty, wet, stinking, black, dangerous work that nearly drove me mad. I worked there for 3 years and saw more horrible things there than I did in my whole time of being a soldier. You always had a chance being a solider, underground there was none, you got swallowed by the earth. Thinking about it sends shivers down my shadow. So being a soldier was always varied. I enjoyed being a soldier and I fitted into army life very well. I liked my pals, you never had better pals than the ones you had in the army, we would have such a laugh and joke together, and you could always rely on them, they never ever let me down. You also got to travelling to new places and seeing new people and their ways, also coming from a poor family I got fed a decent meal which can mean a lot if you have ever suffered from being hungry. I loved the work – protecting places and policing, marching and building, new weapon training - here in the British Army I felt like I belonged. I was not stuck under the ground, feeling free with the sky on top of me.

The third and last thing I need to tell you is that I have discovered something quite by accident. I can write. Big deal I hear you say but it is for me. I never knew I could do this while being a shadow. You see, most things I try and touch just brush through me, like trying to pick up water, you can hold it for a bit but then it's gone. I have tried to ride a bicycle, pick up a cat, have one of them wireless things and press the knobs, pick up pictures, hold someone's hand but nothing.

I tried to read a book, to learn things, even try to understand what was happening to me. I tried to turn the pages when they had been left open but could not move the page. I even tried blowing on it, but nothing. So, I read books and newspapers that are left open. The only thing I can pick up is food but there is not much else you can do with that apart from eating it or staring at it a while. Not so long ago I believed I could not write. I had tried many times to pick up a pencil before because one of my hobbies was drawing. I liked to draw just silly little things like people I knew but I would give them funny faces, or animals with personalities, they were probably very childlike, but I liked to do them anyway. So, it would have been a blessing if I could draw, would have helped pass the time. Then a few months ago someone unaware accidentally dropped a pen, so I went to pick it up and I could hold it. I was so surprised I dropped it. Then picked it up again and have been carrying it ever since. The pen I am writing this with is a different one, you see as soon as I could hold the pen that was dropped I went and tried to see if I could pick up other things, but so far only pens and blank paper. I went into a shop that sold lots of pens and spent hours just picking them up. Feeling something solid in my hand was such a strange experience after all this time. I started to write. At first just my name, then the name of my girl, my Mam and father, names of my friends, the place where I was born, where I lived, the school I went to for a bit, the teacher that taught me. I then wrote about all I could see now, the forest of trees, how people dressed and how they treated each other, rain, what cars were like, how the sun rose, and the birds sang. I wrote for what felt like days and then I slept. When I woke up again, I read what I had written and started to wonder what else I could write about. Not once had I mentioned the war and fighting and being a soldier and I started to wonder why. I had seen so many things, experienced so much during my short life I started to believe that this is why I had been given this ability, so I could write it all down, people would know about everything that happened to me, I had been given a chance to tell my story and maybe, just maybe, this might help leave the world and go where ever all those that I loved have gone to, all those people that I shared my time with on this soil have gone to.

This is my story, of a boy who grew up fast, found a job that he loved, fought in a war that changed everything and still wonders this earth trying to understand what the hell happened to him and the world. By the way my name is Jack Owen Evans. My friends call me Jack.

Corpses in the Undergrowth

Don't let anyone tell you that the fight to take Mametz Wood during July 1916 was anything other than seeing and being part of hell on earth. The days of the actual actions were the 7th, 10th and 11th July, when we the men of the 38th (Welsh) Division fought to the death for every single inch of those woods. Most of us were young, raw recruits, going into action for the first time. There was no point in our officers telling us that it would be a walkover as the events of the previous weeks' actions had dispelled that myth. Just short of 20,000 men had died and 40,000 had been wounded on the 1st July.

Young boys, the cream of their generation had been assured that all the German soldiers would either have been killed or too shocked to even fight. All they had to do was to walk, not run or to rush, but walk forward and we would easily capture the enemy's positions, paving the way for the big break through.

I was a young man then, only 20 years old. I fought there because I had to. It was a case of me or them. Did I actually kill anybody? I don't know. Fleeting glances of field grey uniform would bring my rifle to my shoulder and I'd fire away. But I never stayed upright for long. Fire and drop we were told and that is what I did. The wood was a complete mess. Blasted trees leaning at all angles, with the floor of the wood being a mayhem of undergrowth, broken branches and discarded equipment. The conditions were appalling, but that was nothing in comparison with the sights, sounds and smells that surrounded us. Bodies, ours and theirs, were everywhere. Tree trunks, seemingly painted crimson, but in reality, was the result of being washed with blood – ours and theirs. That was bad, but there were further obscenities to endure.

Body parts decorated the trees and undergrowth. A leg flung up into a tree, still with its boot on, hung there. Headless corpses vividly displaying the contents of the now disappeared head, decorated the front of uniforms. And then a scene so horrible you would have thought that it could only have been conjured up by an artist – but it wasn't. A small Welsh soldier and a seemingly giant of a German soldier, joined in death. They had bayoneted each other at exactly the same moment and were now locked in a surreal death pose. All these sights awaited me as I flew in an instant from being an innocent soldier to a battle-hardened veteran.

All these sights have lived with me for over 70 years, but there is one sight that stays with me, sleeps with me, walks with me constantly. I had taken shelter behind a fallen tree and as lay there I could see the body of a young German soldier, partly covered by undergrowth and debris, lying just ahead of me. His face was whiter than the most perfect marble, yet he had such an innocent, peaceful look about him. I found I couldn't take my eyes off him. What had he done to deserve such a fate; a fate that could come my way at any moment? His eyes were wide open and looking straight at me. They were a striking grey colour staring out as if looking for someone to come and help him, but no amount of help would make him fit and well again. He seemed to be unmarked, except for a faint trickle of blood coming from the corner of his mouth. Did he suffer? Did he die in agony? Were his last words obscenities or did he die

87

calling for his mother. What would she say if she could see him now? I can remember earth being cascaded down onto him, a result of a shell bursting nearby and thinking 'that's not right, he shouldn't be abused any further.' His time was over. Let him lay there in peace.

We were ordered forward again and for me to go forward I had to cross over some of the undergrowth that was covering him. I tried not to look at him, but I found this impossible. It was only when I clambered over the debris that covered him that I realised that he was not whole. I had been looking at his head and upper torso and it was now obvious that this was the sum total of his remains. As I moved, I must have disturbed the undergrowth or some pieces of wood that he had been lying up against, because as I stepped forward his head rolled over and to my horror he was now looking at me again as I walked away from him. I moved forward, my head pulled down into my chest in the nonsensical hope that by adopting this position I would be safe from harm, but even so I could still feel his eyes burning into my back.

The decision as to whether I should look back at him once again was taken from me, as a few moments later a shell burst caught me. It picked me up and shook me about as terrier would a rat. I don't remember much more, that is until I was being carried back to the nearest Regimental Aid Post. My shoulder had copped it but at least I was alive, not like that poor soul now somewhere back there. I was eventually evacuated to a hospital back in England

and took no further part in that insane butchery. The rest is history.

I had no wish to return to the scenes of my youth, but by one way or another my grandsons cajoled me into visiting some of the First World War battlefield areas with them. They brought me to Mametz Wood. The now re-grown wood was green, lush, swathed in birdsong and drenched in sunshine, but for me it was different. When I closed my eyes, I saw a different wood. A thousand emotions washed over me, visions of 1916 came flooding back and there in front of my grandsons I broke down and sobbed uncontrollably. The tears came as if an attempt to exorcise my demons, but no amount of exorcism would clear my mind of what I could still see. He was there again, looking at me and for the first time I realised that he also had had tears in his eyes.

Tears for the 1st July 1916

Hans Richter reached for a stub of indelible pencil. In the wobbly, ill formed, writing of the old or the exhausted, he scrawled the words he had mentally composed, recomposed time after time. Now he sought out the words he had silently mouthed and scrawled his obituary.

31st June 19.00 hrs.

We are in the sixth day of hell. Six days, during which I have been unable, unwilling, to write. The drumfire, the music of the guns and the massive shuddering, rolling and vibrating, rhythm of huge bursting artillery shells, is four metres above us. Continuous, unending, unrelenting. My ears scream, my brain reels, uncontrolled, a mad fandango of disturbed images. I stumble, shake - reach a hand for support at every step. Even the veterans say. "There has never been such a bombardment".

It has been impossible to sleep in this reeking grave-pit. We are on the knife edge of sanity; of what men can bear. Grown men, some the age of my father, cry in terror, in befuddlement, and wipe tears of anguish. No supplies have come forward for days. Bottled water is gone. We are reduced to licking condensation from the broken, splintered wooden bunker walls and roof. Animals. My throat burns. Food? Food is unimportant. Survival, and water, these are the rewards we seek for purgatory.

My dearest, my most trusted, friend Paul Farbe, with me at university, who enlisted and suffered the bestiality of training with me, is broken. The joy, the humour with which he infected us is gone. Gone forever perhaps. He lays, hands bound for his own safety, weeping, screaming. Terror. At each shell burst he contorts in pain and fear. He screams defiance at that which has overwhelmed spirit and his humanity. Can those who survive this hell ever recover from this examination by God?

Even the veterans, those that helped us young soldiers, who fathered us, involuntarily twitch. Continually they look upward, to left, to right, seeking to judge the distance of each shell burst, the fall of shot. Mostly they remain silent, resigned to crucifixion, brooding. No longer can they say, "This is nothing. You should have been with us in 14 when we assaulted Ypres". "This is nothing. When we were at Loos ..." "At Neuve Chapelle we..."

Will we live to direct the same degree of scorn, boast experience, to the many reinforcements needed to bring our company up to strength when – and if - this ever ends? As inspiration I have only the quiet Max Zuber, our machine gun commander. The former farmer has sat, barely moving, virtually silent. For days he has sat, resigned. His thoughts are beyond my understanding. Occasionally he opens one eye, usually the right, his keen sighting eye, and scans the room. He checks us all, offers a cynical smile to us. He closes his eye. At times he lifts his soft cap, fingers the badge, sweeps his fingers over his belt buckle, over the words God With Us. Is he? Is God with us? Like us, does he crave sleep? Does he dream? Did his son enjoy such fear at Calvary? I have no idea. I can no longer face my God.

On the hour, Lieutenant Graz orders: "Two men up".

They stagger to duty above, watching no man's land. Is Tommy finally coming? Frequently only one, and sometime neither, returns. Only we of the Maxim detachment avoid this duty. We are needed when the assault begins we are artists of death, we are more valuable than infantrymen, the simple artisans of killing, more numerous, more dispensable, in the industrial state that is war.

As I write, two of my comrades are lifting the heavy Maxim. Again, they will check its mechanism, clean the chalk which has fallen from the roof. It must be perfect. It must be clean, bright, lightly oiled. We serve the gun, both in action and in rest. We serve the gun and its hunger.

How does one truly describe this terror? Many will try. They will seek to explain this death, choosing precise words, heaping adjective upon adjective to create a picture. They will fail. This, terror, the unbalancing of the mind, the distortion of bodies, the thirst, is incapable of replication on paper. And after? After the barrage lifts and man faces man in technological execution? How will they describe this...?

Hans Richter stood, straight-backed, still, unblinking. Beside him his son, named for Peter Farbe, and his much-loved grandson. He was wary, German visitors to the Somme, the vast graveyard of the British Army, were rare in 1966. They remain so now.

With the remnant of a trench map, now 50 years old, he stood, silent, watching. In the warmth of the early sun, his son holding one hand, his grandson the other, they stood unmoving. He had located his company's approximate position overlooking the gently undulating hill of what the English had called Mash Valley. In the distance, from the huge Lochnagar Crater, blown in the early hours of July 1st 50 years, ago he heard the bugle. Music? No, the strident tones of Last Post for the pilgrims standing by the earth-scar crater. It was now owned by an Englishman, bought to ensure its preservation and as memorial. Far beyond stood the outline of the huge Albert Basilica. The once leaning and damaged statue, the Golden Virgin, which had hung precariously from its roof, now stood erect. Renewed.

"The English", he said, "had believed that only when it fell, collapsed into the rubble below, would the war end. They were almost right. It fell in April 1916 during our final, wasted, efforts to prevent the war being lost" he whispered.

Now, and silently, Hans Richter's tears welled... Burning tears for himself, more for his comrades. They welled for Farbe, who survived the day, insane, to be become subject of the Nazi euthanasia programme as valueless to society. They ran for the strong calm Zuber, who never returned to his farm, his children. For Lieutenant Graz, who died with, and for, his beloved machine guns. He cried for them all, some remembered, others now mere memory-shadows.

Finally, he reached into a pocket, pulled out a small broken-backed journal, the only one which had survived the bombing of Dresden. From its mud stained pages, he began to read the entry for June 31st 1916 aloud. An emotional wall broke anew as he read. He was frequently forced to stop, to wipe his eyes, to take grip. His son and the young boy, his son's only child watched him. They grasped his hand tighter, squeezed tighter. Peter placed his arms round his father's shoulders. As he came to the end of the passage, embarrassed at Opah's pain, they remained silent.

Finally, Peter broke the spell. "Papa, I had no idea. You have never spoken of war, this horror".

"I have put it to the back of my mind", he said.

"It is in a box with all that followed. Post war starvation, inflation, the Nazi Party, the bombing and the camps", he added, eyes lowered, knowing the lie; the lie that stole from the box secretly in the dark night as he lay alone, unsleeping, sweating, frightened anew, untrusting his God.

"On that day, on July 1st 1916, our machine guns murdered thousands of young English, as they had sought to murder us. Young men, mere boys, died in swathes. We had survived. Survived to serve our guns".

Printed in Great Britain
by Amazon